THE MASTERY OF NETWORK MARKETING SALES

LEADS
CUSTOMERS
SALES

A beginners guide to Earning 7 Figures in 6 Months

MAKINDE AYODELE

The Mastery of Network Marketing Sales - Leads Customers Sales

A beginners guide to Earning 7 Figures in 6 Month

The Lifeblood of Every business is sales. What happens to a Network Marketer who has been stockpiling Monthly products without sales? Feelings of Frustration, Nobody wants my Products, Feelings of being used.

This was the situation I found myself in. Imagine having 1.230Million Naira($1000) worth of Supplements and your Bank account is in the Deep Red Zone(2-5k Naira) ($2). Food stuff? Nahhhh!!!!!!. I have more Supplements than foodstuffs. Sad Sad.

Although, I have been selling for over 2 years Now. My decision to sell like a pro 6 months ago (June 2023), understanding the Right audience begging for my products has led to over 6 Figures in Profits.

THE MASTERY OF NETWORK MARKETING SALES - LEADS CUSTOMERS SALES

October Sales

Tre-en-en Qty 3(Maxime P, USA) ======# 164,589

Arthritis solution 4 in 1 Tre-en-en, calmag, full motion, Salmon oil(Marissa S, USA) ====#111,239

Masculine Herbal (Onyenwe Pius, USA) =======# 59,927   **TOTAL = 337,755**

Calmag(#2000 worth, 21 tablets).. Mrs oluwakemi, ibadan =======#2000

November Sales

Tre-en-en qty 3(Maurice maurice, usa) ========= #128,490

Masculine Herbal qty 3(K R Ostrowski, USA) ======#148,290

Tre-en-en + Full motion (Guezere S, USA) ===== #133,261

Full Motion (F Watson, UK) =========# 57,000   **TOTAL= 668,745**

Tre-en-en qty 1 (Juana G, USA) =====#76,556

Neolife Infertility solution 4 products Tre-en-en, chelated zinc, ferminine herbal,calmag (Gonzalez C, USA) ===== #125,148

December Sales

Arthritis solution 4products Tre-en-en, salmon oil, calmag, full motion(Guzman E, USA) =====#126,700

Tre-en-en Qty 6 (Samuel T, USA) =======#272,524   **TOTAL = #623,622**

Tre-en-en Qty 5 (Victorine D, USA) ======#224,398 (Deposit made, total expected after Delivery by Monday)

Forwarded to a third party agent

December, 23 2023 11:37 Local time, FRANKLIN PARK, IL - USA

Origin Service Area : IBADAN - NIGERIA

Destination Service Area : FRANKLIN PARK, IL - USA

Estimated Time of Arrival

December, 28 2023 - By End of Day

Wednesday **December, 20 2023** 21:14 Local time	△	Arrived at DHL Sort Facility LAGOS - NIGERIA LAGOS - NIGERIA
18:45 Local time	△	Shipment has departed from a DHL facility IBADAN - NIGERIA IBADAN - NIGERIA
17:59 Local time	△	Processed at IBADAN - NIGERIA IBADAN - NIGERIA
16:03 Local time	△	Shipment picked up IBADAN - NIGERIA

This book is in 3 Parts to help beginners and sales enthusiast

Part One — Preparing for Sales

Getting prepared for Sales goes beyond having a Product, Introductions to Understanding your Audience, Their interests and how to understand their pain points. Beliefs about sales and understanding the Statistics will be shown and more.

Bonus — How sales Happen

Part Two — Marketing your Products

Where to sell, How to sell and make Massive Profits. Introductions to Advanced Facebook Ads setup, Audience Targeting, Sales Scripts, Cold Calling scripts, how to sell to Strangers, Friends & Neighbors, Trust credibility, Selling with your Website.

Part Three —- The Automated Sales Machine and Sales Challenge

Learn how to automate Sales Process from the Comfort of our Home, Office and many more.

The focus here is setting up the sales process while you focus on other important

This book is only for Individuals ready to take and Implement every step in this book.

Book Launch: March 26, 2024

Pre-Launch Price =
Launch Price:

TABLE OF CONTENT

Tableof Content_____	5
Copyright_____	6
Dedication_____	7
How to Use the Book_____	8
Introduction_____	9
Chapter One_____	11
CHAPTER TWO_____	13
CHAPTER THREE_____	16
CHAPTER FOUR_____	18
CHAPTER FIVE_____	22
CHAPTER SIX_____	29
Conclusion_____	30

COPYRIGHT

© 2024 by Makinde Ayodele Yusuff.

All rights reserved. No part of this publication may be reproduced, distributed, or transmitted in any form or by any means, including photocopying, recording, or other electronic or mechanical methods, without the prior written permission of the publisher, except in the case of brief quotations embodied in critical reviews and certain other noncommercial uses permitted by copyright law.

For permission requests, write to the publisher, addressed "Attention: Permissions Coordinator," at the address below.

Makinde Ayodele Yusuff

ayodele.makinde7@gmail.com

DEDICATION

To every aspiring entrepreneur who dares to dream and takes action to make those dreams a reality. Your passion and perseverance are the driving forces behind the success of your ventures. This book is dedicated to you.

HOW TO USE THE BOOK

Mastering the Art of Sales" is structured to guide you through the intricate landscape of sales, offering practical insights and actionable steps at every turn. Here's how you can make the most of this book:

1. **Start with the Basics**: Begin with Chapter One, "Getting Prepared for Sales," to establish a solid foundation. Understanding the essentials is crucial before diving into more complex strategies.
2. **Follow the Sequence**: Each chapter builds on the previous one. Follow the sequence to ensure you grasp the concepts thoroughly. Skipping around might lead to missing critical connections between different aspects of sales.
3. **Apply the Concepts**: Each chapter includes actionable steps and examples. Take the time to apply these to your own business. Practice makes perfect, and real-world application will solidify your understanding.
4. **Use the Examples**: The examples provided in the chapters, such as the high blood pressure supplement and premium table water, are there to illustrate the principles in action. Relate these examples to your own products or services to see how the strategies can be adapted.
5. **Reflect on the Questions**: Throughout the book, you'll find questions designed to make you think deeply about

your product, audience, and sales strategy. Take the time to answer these questions honestly and thoroughly.
6. **Implement Step-by-Step Guides**: Chapters like "Marketing Your Products" and "Automated Sales" provide step-by-step guides for specific sales techniques and platforms. Follow these guides closely to set up your marketing and sales processes effectively.
7. **Review and Revise**: Sales strategies are not one-size-fits-all. Regularly review your sales processes and results, and don't hesitate to revisit the relevant chapters for fine-tuning and additional insights.
8. **Engage with the Community**: If possible, connect with other readers or sales professionals to share insights, experiences, and tips. Learning from others' experiences can provide valuable perspectives and solutions.
9. **Utilize the Appendices and Resources**: If the book includes appendices or additional resources, make sure to use them. These might offer further reading, templates, checklists, or other tools to enhance your sales process.
10. **Stay Consistent**: Sales success doesn't happen overnight. Consistently applying the principles and strategies from this book will yield the best results over time. Keep refining your approach and stay committed to continuous improvement.

By following this guide on how to use the book, you'll maximize your learning and effectiveness, setting yourself up for sustained sales success. Let's embark on this journey together and unlock your full potential in the world of sales.

INTRODUCTION

Welcome to "Mastering the Art of Sales," a comprehensive guide designed to equip you with the knowledge and tools necessary to excel in the world of sales. Whether you are new to sales or looking to refine your skills, this book provides valuable insights into understanding your products, identifying your audience, and effectively reaching and converting them into loyal customers.

Sales are not just about persuading someone to buy a product; it's about understanding and meeting the needs of your customers. This book will walk you through the essential steps to prepare for sales, from comprehending your product or service in-depth to identifying the pain points of your target audience and crafting the perfect sales strategy.

Each chapter is filled with practical advice, examples, and actionable steps that you can implement immediately. By the end of this book, you will have a clear roadmap to not only reach your sales targets but to surpass them and achieve sustainable business growth.

Let's embark on this journey together and unlock your potential in the world of sales.

CHAPTER ONE
Getting prepared for sales

Sales happens as a result of satisfying a need of an Individual who pays in return to enjoy our Services or Products. Essentially Sales happens when we share what we have to offer to a wider audience. We have to understand that not everyone needs our products. Getting prepared for sales; we have to take notes of the Followings;

a. Understanding our Products/ Services
b. Understanding Who our Audience is
c. Understanding why they need our products(their pain points)
d. Understanding the Best way to reach them
e. How to sell to them

A Lot of individuals jump to how to sell to their Audience without Understanding the essential steps (a-e) . Products/services sell not because of how awesome the product is but because it's tailored to the right Audience. Infact, Every product has its Audience; who are dying to get their hands on it. Remember to always sell the Results of your products/Service.

Understanding your Products/Services: Your Products/service is one of the most important steps in preparing for sales. Your Product/service knowledge is what differentiates you from an Amateur and someone who doesn't know what they are doing. Product Knowledge can be gotten from your business Catalogs, Training and via Experience when used. The Top Sales people understand their Product/service in-depth. Starting with a single product/service Knowledge, it takes a while depending on you, time spent on this step is worthwhile and would save you on your way to becoming a Professional.

Understanding Who our Audience is: One of the Most challenging part is understanding who our Audience is, This can be resolved by the following steps

   a. What do they possible do (Job)
   b. Where do they spend time
   c. How will my product help them
   d. What are their Pains
   e. How will your products make them feel afterwards and many more questions

A simple answer to the above questions will help you resolve who your customer is….. Unto the next step

Understanding why they need our products(their pain points): Why people need your product is one Question you should always ask yourself. One way to do this is simply to have a list of the Issues your products solve, Then a Reverse of who needs it.

An Example:
My products solve Arthritis and Rheumatism, Who needs it ,Men and Especially Women (Age 35 and above).

Understanding the Best way to reach them: Simply put, how can i get my products to their face every time of the day until they buy from me or refer to someone that needs it. Once who understands where they usually spend their Time, Social Media (Facebook, Tiktok, Instagram), Locations, Groups, Website Marketplace and many more. Your Activity can simply lead to more results as you begin to target or reach out to them.

How to sell to them: Selling to your Audience becomes easy when you understand exactly What he needs and Why. Starting with his Problems and potential Ones he might face, You craft a solution that leads to your product or service, letting him/her know how fortunate they are to find your products. What happens when they dont trust you.? Use Your Product Testimonials, Your Product Knowledge and your Persuasion skills.

Example:

Arthritis and Rheumatism Ruins Great Moments with Families and Friends.
Let's get you back in great shape to continue the Fun.

Our Product XYZ is designed to help you ....
Get yours today, click/call etc

CHAPTER TWO

Understanding your Audience

What happens to the best business without customers? It becomes a Charity Organisation waiting for the right moment to shut down permanently. Understanding your Audience, their Behavior and possible pain they felt will be the greatest key to your success.

Understanding your Audience is simplified into three simple steps

      a. How do you Audience feel by a Lack of your products
      b. How do they feel after getting your products
      c. What makes them interested in your products
      d. Where is the need for your products the highest

Example: Our Product is a "High Blood Pressure supplement"

How do your audience feel about a lack of your products?
Without access to your high blood pressure supplement, your audience may feel concerned, anxious, and frustrated about their health condition. They might experience worries about potential complications, such as stroke or heart disease, associated with uncontrolled high blood pressure. Additionally, they might feel limited in their ability to manage their condition effectively without the support of your product.

How do they feel after getting your products?

After obtaining your high blood pressure supplement, your audience is likely to feel relieved, empowered, and hopeful about managing their blood pressure effectively. They may experience a sense of control over their health and well-being, knowing that they have a reliable supplement to support their efforts in maintaining healthy blood pressure levels. Improved vitality, reduced stress, and enhanced overall wellness could be among the positive effects they feel after using your product.

What makes them interested in your products?

Your audience is likely interested in your high blood pressure supplement because it offers a natural and effective solution to manage their condition. They may be drawn to the product's ingredients, such as herbal extracts or vitamins known for their blood pressure-lowering properties. Additionally, the promise of reducing dependency on prescription medications or avoiding potential side effects associated with conventional treatments could be compelling factors. Testimonials, scientific evidence, and endorsements from healthcare professionals may also contribute to their interest in your product.

Where is the need for your products the highest?

The need for your high blood pressure supplement is highest among individuals with hypertension or those at risk of developing high blood pressure. This includes middle-aged and older adults, individuals with a family history of hypertension, people with sedentary lifestyles, and those with poor dietary habits. Moreover, regions or communities with limited access to healthcare facilities or where lifestyle-related factors contribute to a high prevalence of hypertension may also have a significant demand for your product.

Another Example: Our product is " Premium Table Water"

How do your audience feel about a lack of your products?

Without access to your premium table water, your audience might feel frustrated, dissatisfied, and concerned about their hydration and overall health. They may perceive tap water or other alternatives as inferior in taste, quality, or purity compared to your premium offering. Furthermore, they might worry about potential health risks associated with consuming water of uncertain quality or with undesirable taste.

How do they feel after getting your products?

After acquiring your premium table water, your audience is likely to feel refreshed, satisfied, and confident in their hydration choice. They may experience a sense of luxury and indulgence, appreciating the superior taste and purity of your water. Knowing they are consuming water that meets the highest standards of quality and safety could instill a feeling of well-being and peace of mind. Additionally, the elegant packaging and branding of your product might evoke feelings of prestige and sophistication.

What makes them interested in your products?

Your audience is likely interested in your premium table water because it offers a superior drinking experience compared to other options available in the market. They may be drawn to the exceptional purity and taste of your water, which is achieved through advanced filtration or purification processes. The premium packaging and branding of your product might also appeal to their sense of aesthetics and desire for sophistication. Furthermore, if your water is sourced from pristine natural springs or unique locations, the story behind its origin could further captivate their interest.

Where is the need for your products the highest?

The need for your premium table water is highest among consumers who prioritize quality, purity, and taste in their hydration choices. This includes health-conscious individuals, discerning consumers with refined tastes, and those who seek a luxurious drinking experience. High-end restaurants, hotels, spas, and gourmet food stores represent key markets where demand for premium table water is likely to be significant. Additionally, regions or countries where concerns about water quality or access to clean drinking water are prevalent may also present opportunities for your product, especially among affluent demographics seeking an alternative to tap water or standard bottled water brands.

Crafting a Sales Copy that Converts

When crafting Sales copy, the Focus is to share a story, everyone loves a story. The Story should be in the Following Format:

    a. Issues/Problems faced before using Product(How they feel)
    b. How they product/service can help solve the problem
    c. How they felt after using the Products

Example

Having Children of my own was a thing I looked forward to before Marriage. It's been two years since my Husband struggled with conceiving a child. I felt shame and had a sad feeling whenever I saw/heard about a neighbor who just gave birth.

12 Months ago, I was introduced to XYZ. I read about its functions and I decided to give it a Trial.

2 weeks ago, I just gave birth to a baby Boy and I am looking forward to another one soon with my husband.

The above example tells a story of someone who used the Products/service to achieve their goals. This type of Example can be in Video Form of Testimony or Content. Just get creative and test around with what works best.

Another Reminder, Don't sell the products, sell the results. Nobody cares about the Ingredients.

CHAPTER THREE

Beliefs about Sales

Here are a list of beliefs individuals have about selling Supplements;

- A. Nobody wants my Products
- B. It's too expensive
- C. Will this products(How effective it is)
- D. How will my Body React to it (Side effect)
- E. I am on Drugs already, Hope this won't lead to more problems for me

NOBODY WANTS MY PRODUCTS

This is one of the most situations individuals think about, Let's do a Quick Analysis and Statistics about health issues worldwide

- a. The number of people living with hypertension (blood pressure of 140/90 mmHg or higher or taking medication for hypertension) doubled between 1990 and 2019, from 650 million to 1.3 billion

- b. About 422 million people worldwide have diabetes, the majority living in low-and middle-income countries, and 1.5 million deaths are directly attributed to diabetes each year.

- c. In 2019, 18 million people worldwide were living with rheumatoid arthritis (1).About 70% of people living with rheumatoid arthritis are women, and 55% are older than 55 years.

d. Worldwide, an estimated 1,414,259 people were diagnosed with prostate cancer in 2020. It is the fourth most commonly diagnosed cancer in the world.

Simply, A Whole lot of individuals need your product, Infact, Anyone that resents your product doesn't need it. Let's assume, you have not had water for 3 days. Someone decides to sell water to you on the fourth day, How will you respond?

Instead of focusing on people that doesnt need your products, continue to explore ways to find individuals who are dying to have your products.

IT'S TOO EXPENSIVE

There is always a Difference between, I can't afford it and it's too Expensive. Most Individuals fall in the I can't afford it but Claim to be expensive.

When someone claims its expensive, Ask them the following Questions
        a. Is this within your Budget?
        b. If you are to get the products Now, What info would you need to Know.
        c. Are you aware of the Benefits of the products
        d. If you are buying now, I am offering you a 10% discount, Price reduction, XYZ. Are you ready to get this offer?.

This and some more questions are what's needed to Qualify your Prospects. You begin to understand exactly what the issue is, maybe its Knowledge about the products, Trust about what the products can do and if its Genuine and Authentic and many more.

More Questions helps you understand and get the customer to buy.

Will this products(How effective it is)

The best way to answer this, is to share the Product Information(pdfs) and Product Testimony. Product Assurance from Nafdac and other Agency. Also, Taking the Product right in the customer presence(a Sample etc). Provide Assurance,.. If this product does not do this in 30 days, I will provide Refund.

How will my Body React to it (Side effect)

All supplements are natural, GMO Free depending on the Company you partner with. Best way to tackle this is to simply Show them the Ingredients on the Products label, letting them know that excess use of any products has effects. The Product label and understanding your products is to key to winning at this objection or issue

I am on Drugs already, Hope this won't lead to more problems for me

Taking Supplements for Individuals who are on a Particular drug, Wait 3 hours after taking the
Drugs they are on before taking supplements. Some supplements interact with some drugs, please do well to ask and do your research.

Understanding how to resolve the Belief and Objections about Products sales will allow you to easily resolve this and make sales .

CHAPTER FOUR

Marketing your Products

Understanding how to market your products is a skill to be developed. Marketing your products simply means ensuring potential customers get to see your products until they make a decision to buy. Here is a list of place to Market your Product

- a. Facebook Ads
- b. Instagram Ads
- c. Ecommerce Marketplace in your Country e.g Ebay, Amazon, Temu, Etsy
- d. Billboard and Banner
- e. Fliers
- f. Personal Ecommerce Website
- g. Product Funnel

The Focus in this Chapter is Facebook Ads, Instagram Ads, Ecommerce Website and Ecommerce Marketplace, step by Step. Other methods highlighted will be discussed too.

FACEBOOK ADS

Facebook Ads consist of three Different parts
- a. The Campaign Level
- b. The Adset
- c. The Ads

The Campaign Level is where you set the Ads Objectives which includes
- a. Awareness
- b. Traffic

c. Engagement
   d. Leads
   e. App promotion
   f. Sales

The Best Objectives for Ads is Sales, as our goal is to Find people who are likely to purchase our product or service.. The Sales objectives have conversions in Website, WhatsApp, Instagram, catalog sales and many more. Our Goals here are to utilize WhatsApp and our Website, each with different strategies and methods that drive sales.

The Adset level is where you set up your Conversion location, Budget, Pixel, Audience and many more. This level also allows you to see the Estimated results and conversions. In cases you see your estimated results not encouraging, it's time to set up your Budget and Audience and other required details.

The Ad Level is where you set up your Ads creative, Facebook Pages and Instagram Pages, CTAs(Call to Actions), Destinations, Headline, Primary text and many more.

Note: When Running Ads for Sales, Run an Awareness ads and a Sales Ads(WhatsApp, Website etc). This is to ensure your Ads converts

Here is a Link to Understand more on Ads Creation for Facebook and Instagram

   https://web.facebook.com/business/learn/courses

INSTAGRAM ADS

Setting up Instagram Ads directly On Instagram, can be simply done using the Following steps

   a. Create a Post on your IG account relating to the content you want to promote
   b. Click on "Boost Post"

c. Select your Goals, this includes; Visit your Profile, Visit your Website and get more messages.
d. Audience, You can select from a list or create new ones. When creating new ones, you are to Name the Audience, Age Range and Locations
e. Budget and Duration,Daily spend and Duration for Ads
f. Boost Post and add your payment method(card or any available in your region)
g. Wait for review and your ads will start running

HOW TO SPY ON COMPETITOR ADS

Spying on competitor Ads is one way to have a clue on how your competitors run ads, Their Contents, Ads Creatives and others. GoTo: https://web.facebook.com/ads/library/. Search for Ads based on any products or company.

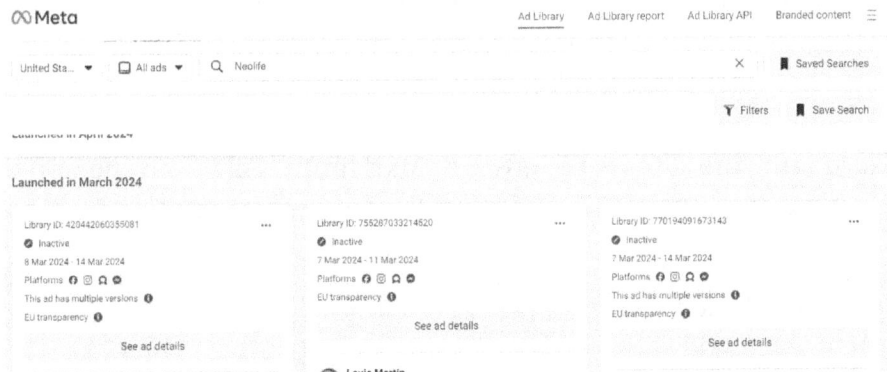

Ecommerce Marketplace is one awesome way to make sales, this is due to the Traffic this website gets on a daily and Monthly. Also, Marketplace has built trust over the years giving the Opportunity to scale up your products sales at any Time. Depending on your Region. Here is a list of the Best Marketplace around the World
  a. Amazon
  b. Ebay
  c. Jumia
  d. Temu

e. Aliexpress
f. Alibaba
g. Bestbuy
h. Walmart
i. Etsy and many more

Billboards and Banner, In commercial Areas across the Globe, Billboards and banners are one of the most important ways to Advertise your products to Everyone all day long. Why is this important? Not everyone is on Social media, your information is passed across to everyone who could probably buy, request more information and also give you free referrals.

This method might seem old , but it's very effective in this busy world where everyone needs quick information.

Personal Ecommerce Website is one of the new effective methods for ensuring maximum sales, remove the fees associated with selling on other Ecommerce and Marketplace,

Here are the Steps to ensure Maximum Sales on personal ecommerce websites. First, Let's talk about where to sale

a. Shopify
b. Wordpress
c. Ecwid
d. Wix
e. Mailchimp
f. Flutterwave
g. Paystack
h. Stripe and many more

Here is the Step to get sales, Personal ecommerce stores needs the followings to generate sales

a. Marketing (Social Media Marketing an others)
b. SEO optimization

c. Build Trust and Testimonials
d. Link up Payment gateways that allows easy payments options for everyone shopping
e. Domain setup, if no free hosting, Domain and hosting which isn't free
f. Product Upload and Store designs and others

Personal ecommerce stores take a whole lot of time and Serious Marketing to get results, getting started requires having the right understanding and models to scale up.

Product Funnels, product funnels is a series of pages guiding a Prospect to make a decision to buy our product, this step is similar to website. Here are softwares you can use

a. Clickfunnels
b. Highlevel
c. Systeme.io and lots more.

Both Funnels and websites require almost the same methods to get results.

Bonus,

Google My Business, Yes Yes...... Considering you live in a neighborhood or close proximity where someone needs your products/services. Searching for your Products/services on Google will automatically show up your business to them with the options to message , call, check directions and buy on your Website.

AYODELEMAKINDE

Google | neolife products near me

All Images Maps Videos News More   Tools

Open now   Akobo, ibadan

About 93 results (0.49 seconds)

Results for **Ward XII, Nw8** ⊙ Use precise location

Locations

A **GNLD/NEOLIFE products and health suppl...**
   Ibadan · 0810 025 9848
   Open 24 hours
   In-store shopping · In-store pick-up · Delivery
   Website   Directions

B **Neolife/GNLD Products In Ibadan**
   Ibadan · 0706 972 9771
   Open 24 hours

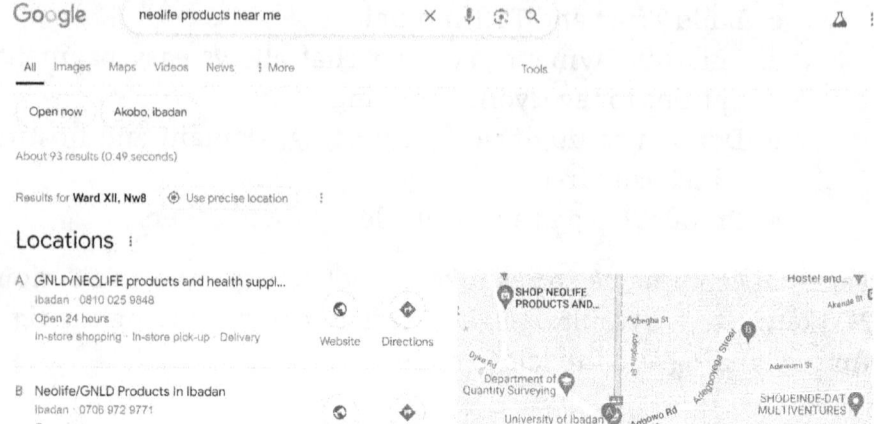

CHAPTER FIVE

Sales RoadMap

The Chapter introduces and focuses on the various proven steps to get results.

Selling to Friends, Neighbors and Family

The Easiest way to sell to this category of Individuals is to carefully explain how the Products you give them works, then share only a few with them. This way, they get to enjoy the benefits and can help you spread the Word. Note: Only give to people who show keen interest in the Products, do not force anyone.

Location Based/ Walk-in

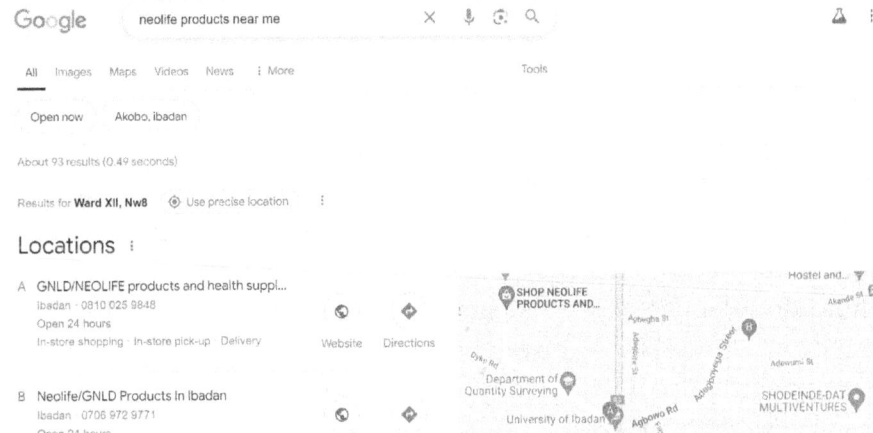

This methods leverages on Google myBusiness and Business address as stated in your Social Media, Website and lots more.

27

Google my business Suggests your business to individuals when there's a match and your business pops up on google. Customers who use the above method are in dire need of your products as they want an Urgent solutions to their Problems/needs.

How to succeed with this method simply means getting ready for sales; that is your sales presentations, Answer their objections, understand how to close sales including giving discounts that won't hurt your profits. For every 10 visit with the Above 90% will convert instantly with 5% buying later on and the rest can't afford your price. To setup your google my business, simply search " Google Mybusiness profile creation and follow the prompt.

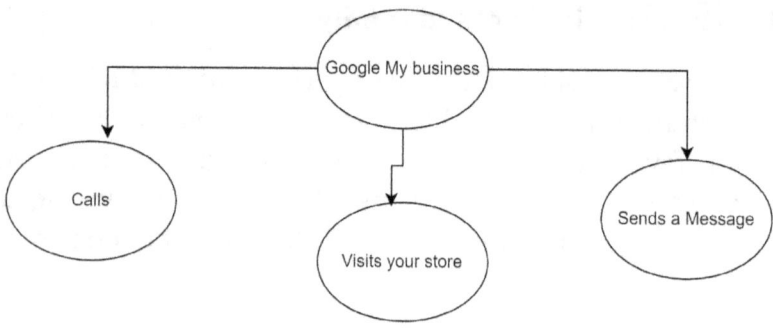

Website

This methods requires Active Marketing via Social media, Referrals, Word of mouth et.c the Success here lies in carefully Crafting a Sales Page or Product Page that converts the Visitor into customers with easy Payments methods and ways to track Abandoned Cart. Most visitors on a website might get distracted or don't understand how the products solves their problems, Issues with Trust and many more. Setting up sales on Website requires lots of efforts.

To solve these issues, is to share your process of when

customers purchase and the steps to delivery, after-sales, Returns, Testimonials and many more.

Essentially, The key to success in this RoadMap is Marketing, Awesome Website design, Awesome Product descriptions, Easy Checkout process and Products Testimonials.

Approximately, 20% of Websites visitors make purchases. More Traffic more Sales

Note: Ensure Facebook Pixel and other forms of Activity Tracking is installed on your website to understand your audience behavior and actions on the Website. Also a Lead capture form offering a free Gift(Ebook, Discount etc) should be available to get leads.

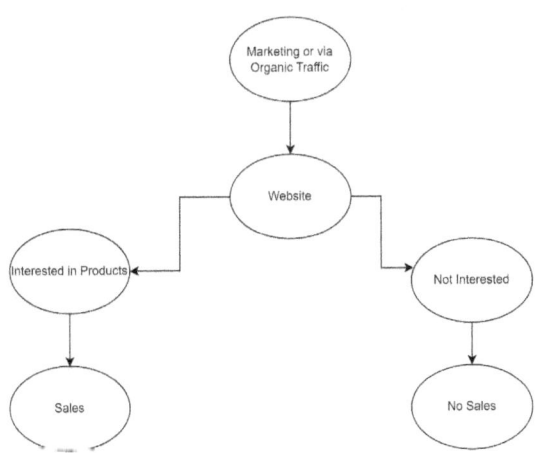

Facebook Groups

Simply run a Marketing campaign on Facebook and get people to join your Facebook Group. Once the Group has reached the Targeted NUmber of Audience, you can start to Educate them, pitch your products and get them to buy over a Two day period and continuous. Note: Video Testimonials convert more in this scenario and it's best you add them to a Broadcast List to constantly Remind them.

Only 20-40% will convert, ensuring you have so many individuals in the group. Weekly Educative Tips is also Encouraged.

You can always do this every month, new set of people, start the process continuously

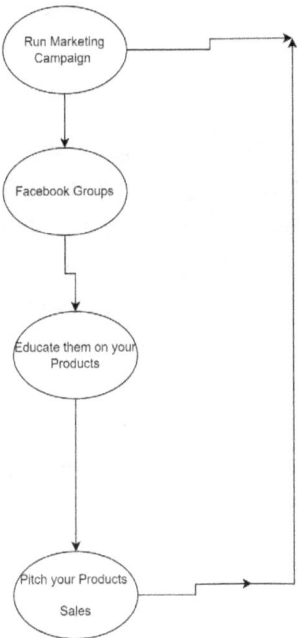

WhatsApp

WhatsApp has over 2 billion users across the World(2024) making it one essential messaging tool in everyday life. One of the Many benefits of WhatsApp is you're able to get in contact with anyone that has messaged you at least once. This includes their Phone Number, Email, Profile Picture and more.

WhatsApp Integration with Facebook Ads Makes it easier for anyone to reach out to you directly from your Ads to ensure easy Communication.

3 steps to convert with WhatsApp Ads

1. Calls (A script will be provided)
2. Messaging (A simple scripts will be provided)
3. Product proof/ A video call showing yourself and products
4. WhatsApp Groups

WhatsApp Groups

Simply run a Marketing campaign on Facebook and get people to join your WhatsApp Group, either by messaging you first, then add them to the group. Once the Group has reached the Targeted NUmber of Audience, you can start to Educate them, pitch your products and get them to buy over a Two day period and continuous. Note: Video Testimonials convert more in this scenario and it's best you add them to a Broadcast List to constantly Remind them.
Only 20-40% will convert, ensuring you have so many individuals in the group. Weekly Educative Tips is also Encouraged.

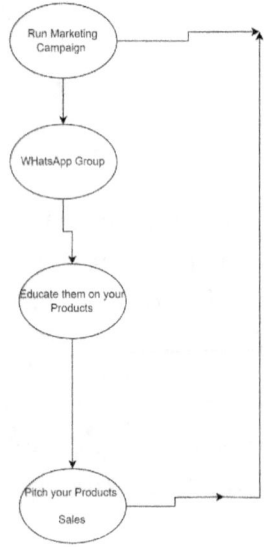

Calls

Whenever, a New Message drops in your WhatsApp. Immediately call them and use the following scripts

"

Good Day Mr/Mrs ...(Their name)..., I am ...(your name)..... Calling you from ....(your company name...). We got your message about your interest in …..XYZ…… That's why we are calling you. How are you today?

We would like to share with you more about the products… However, we would love to hear from you about you interest in this products

.
. Let them talk more(Ask Questions relating to products)
.

Once you understand their Whys and Interest in the products

We are currently offering a 24 hour discount for every product's sales.

If you're buying Now

You will get ……….discount
You will get ………. Free delivery
You will get free XYZ

Ensure your Offers don't hurt your profits

Messaging

First…… A welcome Message e.g Hello, Welcome to XYZ, We pride ourselves in helping individuals achieve quality health with our Top Products, How can we be of service to you today..

"

Build relationships with them, find something you have in common, ask Questions relating to the products they need. Before pitching the Products

When Pitching the Products, always share a Video or PDFs relating to the Products. The video should be a Testimonial or How to use it.

Closing the Sales

Ask them if they need anything extra as regards Informations or questions

Once you've answered their questions and all

Shoot your Shot...

The Products cost .... If you're buying today in the next 24 hours, you will get the following.
.... Add your Discounts and offers.. Ensure it doesn't hurt your profit.

Then follow up after 12 hours with a Product Testimonial Video.

Next 24 hours with Final Offer Message. If they don't buy after, simply follow up once a week with Benefits of the Products.

Video Proof

In most cases, a proof of Quality and to show you're not a scam might require you to go on a Video call with your prospects to explain more about what you do and the products. In this case, It's best you ask the prospect if they would love to join you on a video call to see the products and also understand more. The Closing methods apply.

Selling via WhatsApp Groups

Simply Drive Traffic to your WhatsApp using WhatsApp Ads or Other Organic Methods, Where Individuals Join your WhatsApp Group for the Presentation.

This method requires you to prepare all the materials needed including Medias and others. Best thing to do here is to start from a method of letting the prospects understand the Problems and walk them to the Solutions with your Products/ services. Offer discounts and ensure to follow up on the Rest that are yet to make a buying decision.

Selling with Facebook Live

One of the Best methods of selling via Facebook is Going live to educate people on different topics relating to your products. This method requires consistency and knowledge about what you do. You present a Topic, share more details, make it interactive and then present how your product solves the problem.

An interesting method used by Realtors is to just share information and let the Prospect make the decision to contact them for help.

Selling with Marketplace
This method includes listing your products on the Ecommerce Marketplace. The Top 3 best Marketplaces are Amazon, Etsy and Ebay. Amazon has a Subscription for the First Month, you can change this to Individual Plan which is free. Ebay and Etsy are free to join.

How to List your Products for selling

    a. Only sell Products as a combination not as a Single Products to solve people's health issues.
    b. Only Label the products based on its functionalities
    c. Describe only the Functions of the Products, be honest
    d. Ensure you understand the Pricing for Products to avoid losses. FInd the Pricing calculator for each of the Top Marketplace listed above
    e. Ensure you ship only Quality Products to your customers
    f. Ensure products price is updated on any change (increase or decrease)
    g. Use only a quality shipping company

CHAPTER SIX

Automated Sales

Automated Sales comes from Having multiple Sales Channels that drive sales every month. It simply means even if one's sales channel doesn't convert others will.

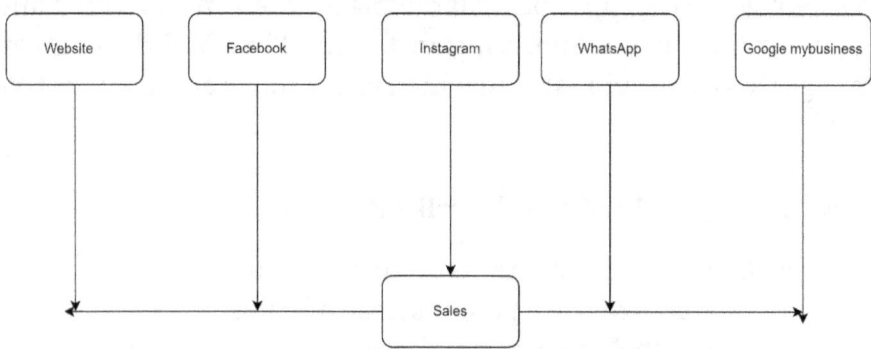

It starts with achieving results with Methods, Scale it up, Repeat the process. Then start working on others. Meanwhile, Not everyone can scale up via the methods above. Simply stick with what gets you results.

CONCLUSION

As we conclude "Mastering the Art of Sales," it is important to reflect on the journey we have taken together. You have learned the fundamental principles of preparing for sales, understanding your audience, addressing common beliefs and objections, and effectively marketing your products. These insights are designed to empower you to approach sales with confidence and a strategic mindset.

Remember, the key to successful sales lies in understanding your customers' needs and continuously refining your approach to meet those needs. Sales is not a one-time event but an ongoing process of building relationships, trust, and delivering value.

Keep experimenting with different strategies, learning from your experiences, and staying adaptable in the ever-changing market landscape. With the knowledge and tools gained from this book, you are now well-equipped to drive your business towards success.

Thank you for choosing to enhance your sales skills with this guide. Wishing you all the best in your sales endeavors and future business ventures.

www.ingramcontent.com/pod-product-compliance
Lightning Source LLC
Chambersburg PA
CBHW050251230526
45470CB00005B/2217